MAVIS MALCOLM

RELATIONSHIP CURE

The Ultimate Guide to Stronger and Better Relationships,
Discover Useful Tips and Ways on How to Maintain and
Nurture All Your Relationships

Descrierea CIP a Bibliotecii Naționale a României
MAVIS MALCOLM
    **RELATIONSHIP CURE. The Ultimate Guide to Stronger
and Better Relationships, Discover Useful Tips and Ways on
How to Maintain and Nurture All Your Relationships** / Mavis
Malcolm. – Bucharest: Editura My Ebook, 2020
    ISBN 978-606-983-587-6

MAVIS MALCOLM

RELATIONSHIP CURE

The Ultimate Guide to Stronger and Better Relationships, Discover Useful Tips and Ways on How to Maintain and Nurture All Your Relationships

My Ebook Publishing House
Bucharest, 2020

TABLE OF CONTENTS

CHAPTER 1

THE BASICS ON FRIENDSHIPS

Synopsis

"No Man Is an Island", this line extracted from Meditation XVII, by an English poet John Donne has been a very popular expression when talking about people's connection from one another. Indeed, there is nobody who can live alone on this planet. That is why God created different form of relationships, such as friendship. Friendship is one of the greatest forms of relationship that everyone will surely want to have.

To be able to understand what friendship is, you must look at its definitions and reasons for its importance and goodness. For this, you can refer to the great and famous philosopher Aristotle.

A lot of philosophers give emphasis on conjecture and theory. For sure, Aristotle has contributed to this kind of philosophy as well. He has given great emphasis on the reasons why friendship is essential.

The Basics

According to him, no one will ever opt to live without friends. This notion from Aristotle is indeed very significant because he emphasizes that even though people with all other possessions, being really rich and having offices and holding dominating power are considered to be, most of all in need of friends.

He even added that what would be the use of those prosperities without having the chance to beneficence that can be practiced mainly and on its most worthy form to friends. Aside from being able to beneficence, friends will help you guard and preserve your prosperity. Friends are more worthy and beneficial to men in misfortunes and in poverty, for they can consider their friends as their only refuge.

"Friendship is as important as life itself", this is a statement given by Aristotle powerful and bold. Friendship covers old and young, poor and rich. It covers the breath of the kinds of people you find within the society.

In fact, rich men are considered to need friends the most, for being rich contains no value except when they have someone or some people to share their wealth with. Not to mention about the fact that friendship can definitely reduce risk.

This should be true because when the time comes that you meet an unexpected occurrence, you can always seek some assistance from your true friends. This results to unfortunate men who could benefit from friends during the time of misfortune and poverty.

However, most importantly from all other facts is that friendship could stimulate a person to righteous actions. By joining with your friends, you will be able to have favorable thoughts and act accordingly. There is always something really special with the feeling of friendship making you desire to act. A person should acquire that sense of delight whenever giving assistance to his friends although it is not usually a joyful task. With friends you always give the best shot of everything you are sharing together.

With this idea, you can already think that friendship improves your life because it makes you a better individual. In trying to serve your friends, you always get to benefit from it by improving yourself. These facts alone could offer you what it gets to have your friends around and to build the most trustworthy friendship.

CHAPTER 2

IDENTIFY WHERE YOUR FRIENDSHIPS
HAVE ISSUES

Synopsis

Making and keeping good friends is indeed a great thing to consider. Both or all of you share laughter and tears during your life. However, it can never be avoided to have issues of your friendships. Yes, it can give you the worth feelings when you are facing issues with your friends. That is why knowing and understanding where your friendships have issues is very important. If you know the reasons behind these issues, it will become easy for you to resolve them.

It is almost as difficult to simplify friendship issues as it is identify how to resolve them. There are a few issues that might sound similar or contain particular elements in common, yet in terms of going about the details; each friendship contains a unique trajectory in accordance to the different mix of circumstances, history and personalities.

Where Are There Issues

Whenever a serious issue crops up with your friends, it is normally disappointing, unexpected, and very inconvenient to deal with. The main key to dealing with these issues is communication. However, at most times, many people are at loss of the things to say or to move forward during a sticky situation.

There are different situations where friendship issues may arise. Time is one of the most essential elements of maintaining a good friendship.

However, when you or your friend is very busy with his work or any other related factors, issues might not be avoided to arise. This is especially painful if you are used to seeing each other. If your friend is too busy with work, you won't be sure if you could count on him/her during hard times or when you have something special to attend. This can put some stains on your friendship. If you wish to fix such kind of issue, it will be very helpful to let your friend know how you feel about your situation. Let him/her know that you are upset. Considering this may give some ideas to your friend on what to do if he/she really wishes to treasure what both of you have. With this, you can at least make your friend aware by being honest to him/her of what you feel.

Another issue that might arise on friendship is having and living separate lives when in fact both used to be attached at the hip. It could be very unusual if you and your friend were once very attached to each other and yet now don't know the rights words to utter. Both of your lives might have gone so different that your friendship is not what it really once was.

Friendship has its ups and downs, and some of them may last forever. Know if it possible for you to identify what is wrong by having talk with your friend about it. If there is something about her, you or perhaps both of you have changed; you can try maintaining a distant connection and not completely cutting off your friendship.

Feeling that your friend has deserted you without giving any explanation is another major issue between friends. This can possible bring your friendship to an end without knowing the reason behind. Having to meet this kind of situation, of course, you will want a closure. When your friendship has declined, it will be a good idea if you and your friend get a common knowledge about the thing that happened and the reason behind it, yet this is not always possible.

Usually, friends might not provide you such opportunity. This kind of issue about friendship will usually root from something you have done or said to your friend that you don't actually mean, yet taken by your friend in a wrong way. If your friend is just too coward or timid to tell his/her reasons fixing the problems can really be hard. However, you are the one who should persuade him/her so as to fix it. Convince him/her that your friendship is truly valuable to you and that you don't want to lose it.

Fixing your issues in the shortest period of time must be considered. So, make sure to keep that valuable friendship by knowing and avoiding your possible issues with your friend.

CHAPTER 3

HOW YOUR FRIENDSHIPS AFFECT YOUR LIFE

Synopsis

Just about every individual is aware that his friends could affect his life in one way or another. However, most people are just not aware that such effect could be most influential than they could ever imagine. Your friends do not only influence you when making your decisions, they can also change how you view the world, alter your insight and change you into the different person.

The Impact

Your friends can really influence you, so you should know about the ways how. Friends can indeed alter your beliefs of things. Beliefs and values could be a changed when they are constantly challenged and when new beliefs are constantly repeated.

For instance, if you have a circle of friends who have a negative view of the employment market even before they had the opportunity to work with it, it can also affect you. Such pessimistic view probably came from the constant idea they obtained from friends in the form of suggestions which are repeated again and again, such as "it is very hard to search for a job nowadays".

Your friends could affect your self-confidence. Friends have the capability to change the perception of one another. When the majority of your group is thinking that a certain person is snobbish and arrogant, this belief may be transferred to the entire group.

While believing that a person is treating you in an unfavorable way, you might interpret it being a sign showing that you're not really worthy. Such belief may badly affect the level of your self-confidence.

Your friends can also affect the way you behave. Being very attached to your friends can also affect your behavior. For instance, if you see that your friend is polite to someone, particularly old, even when you are not you can think that doing such thing is indeed a delightful thing.

This will then let you do the same. In addition to affecting your beliefs, your friends can also affect how you react of things. For instance, you are initially not afraid of snakes, yet after you know how it affects your friend beaten by it, your point view and behavior should you see one will also change. This is how influential friendship could be.

Your friends could stir you with good and bad emotions. Depending on the type of friends you are joining with, your emotions can be greatly affected by them. If you have friends who are jolly at most times, you can observe yourself to be jolly around them as well. Of course, if you care about your friends you will feel sad whenever they are sad.

This is how really the transference of emotions within friendship gets. But then, if you don't want to feel as sad as your friend, letting him feel good by giving him positive advice of his situation should be a great idea. Letting your friend know and feel that you care can really lift up his mood. This is completely how friends affect you, and it greatly depends on you if you will them rule on how you feel, think and belief.

CHAPTER 4

WHAT MAKES A GOOD FRIEND?

Synopsis

There are different types of friends. There is the good and the bad. However, who will want to be with bad friends? Probably, no one will want to. So, if you want your friends to be good to you, you have to make sure that you are good to them as well.

There are three types of friendship. These include friendship of virtue, friendship of mutual interest and friendship of usefulness. Whatever types of friend you have, it is still imperative for you to be a good friend.

So, what makes a friend a good friend? It is important that you don't just know the qualities of a good friend. You must also know how to act and be like one. If you are a good friend, you will rejoice in your friend's joys and will sorrow over his pains. A good friend is not only sympathetic, he is also empathetic. You will share his feelings, weeping with him when he weeps and rejoice with him when he rejoices. A good friend won't defriend his friend is he disagrees. Friendships should be tested whenever there are some disagreements. Yet, if you are a good friend you will never cut your friends off for that reason. You will tell them what you think they need to hear and the other way around. However, you must do it in a way you know they can accept it. You may do this if you really love them unconditionally more than you care for your views.

A Good Friend?

A good friend will always keep in touch with you regularly. You can contact your friends from time to time and you can expect that they will do the same to you. Friends like these are regarded as good friends. So, if you consider yourself as a good friend, you must communicate with your friends fairly regularly. Trust is a very important element of friendship.

Knowing that you can trust your friend and that your friend trusts you are indeed a joyful thing. A good friend can be trusted implicitly. You must earn the trust of your friend and yours to them. Consequently, you need not to doubt that they will have your back. This will also eliminate the fear of your friends stabbing in your back. If you trust your friends enough you won't hesitate to reveal them about your highly confidential and private matters.

A good friend should defend and stand by your side should bad times take place. This is probably the topmost measure of friendship. Being a good friend, you will feel what your friend is feeling. It is like "hurting my friend, means hurting me". It should not come out as, "well, you don't do anything to me, so it is not my issue". If you give care to your friend, you will stand by him during such tough battles. Instead of further worsening the situation, you may at least calm her by giving her positive outlooks. Making the situation worse by fighting the same person who has hurt your friend will never be a good idea. This only means that a good friend does not promote convoluted situations, but rather make things right in the proper way he knows how to.

CHAPTER 5

WHAT MAKES A BAD FRIEND?

Synopsis

Of course, if there is a good friend, expect that there is always the bad. That is why you have to be very careful when choosing or staying with your supposed "friends". Finding out the difference between a good and bad friendship is not as simple as it might look.

On the other hand, there are a number of ways you could tell a friendship is not good.

There are times when you will find it hard to think about the things you will do with your "not really" good friends, and ending it can sometimes be your only choice.

Getting some assistance should you need some is truly an important part of guaranteeing that you are surrounded by true people.

Bad Friend?

Sometimes, a friendship might confuse you - you won't be sure who among them are really loyal, genuine and supportive. Hence, you must know how to spot those bad friends. You certainly want to be wary about those opportunists.

An opportunist is the person who only likes to be with you because he wants to use you for your assets, such as your car, home or apartment. Or perhaps, he might be using you in order to become close to your well-off friends or sibling.

This kind of person might consume your home or house and maybe even utilize your private hygiene products. Yet, when you confront him, he becomes angry at you. This only shows his disrespect to you and your belongings. Being wary about this kind of person must be observed.

Another trait of a bad friend is being self-centered. This kind of person is living by the tune "it is completely about me". These people always talk of themselves.

They won't also give care about you, being uninterested of what you do in a day, the way you feel and more. You might also observe of them always taking big. Whether it is about themselves, boyfriend/girlfriend, materialistic possessions, a vacation, or getting married, this type of people always find the thing that will make them look better than you. Friends with this kind of attitude could be hard to trust and keep.

On the other hand, having a friend who always seems to pity on himself is also not a good trait of a friend. This is the type of person who will always come to you whenever he is facing a problem and seeking for some advice. They will let you know about the difficulties they are going through letting you feel pity for them. But then, if you are the one who needs help from them, they will fall short on you. It won't be fair if you do not mind spending 2 hours just to give them composure, yet it is like they find it hard to give their five minutes to you. You are not their therapist, so you should avoid letting them broadcast their moans on your expense.

Spotting bad friends is just so easy, yet only if you are sensitive enough to feel what they are up to. Trusting these days is not that easy, so you should be careful to whom you will offer it.

CHAPTER 6

LEARN TO UNDERSTAND PEOPLE BETTER

Synopsis

Having a friend is not as easy as what you may think at all times. Being a friend to your friend sets some responsibilities that you need to fill in. If you want your friendship to last as long, you need to care and understand one another. Whether you have just met your friend, or has know him/her since the good old days, he will always do something which may slope your keel, forcing you from asking yourself, "how well do I truly know this person?"

Understanding

Asking this question, you will surely do something to figure out how you can understand your friend better. If you wish to know those people you call friends better, you will take your chance to know their families as well as other friends personally. By doing this, you will get the chance to know the types of people they interact with. You will also get to discover their closeness to their families. So, you may ask your friends if you can come to their house meeting their family and spending quite some time with other friends. When they hesitate, keep note to give them some time. You can spend some time with your friends before deciding to barge in into their personal lives.

Making a discussion about their obsessions in a fine manner may also do the trick. In this way, your friends should be grateful of your interest. You'll get to know the things that make them tick and with them to you, vice versa.

Knowing their likes and dislikes should give you better understanding of your friends. Digging too much might not be advisable. Make sure not to force them to talk with their personal lives. You may open and ignite the topic yourself and let them freely open and talk about them. This should provide you comfortable and worry-free conversation. Understanding your friends is indeed important in building a better and more dependable friendship, so make sure to keep a note of these ideas, as it may help you achieve whatever it is you want to achieve.

CHAPTER 7

THE BENEFITS OF FRIENDSHIPS

Synopsis

Having friends around could be very delightful. Friendship is actually one of the most precious relationships a person can ever treasure, so make sure you keep the friendships you presently have most especially the good ones. Spending quite some time with good friends is extremely gratifying for a lot of people and it can provide you some shocking side effects. Your friends do not only improve your self-esteem and mood, yet it also decreases stress and lessens your risk of experiencing terminal illness.

Keeping track with friendships could be difficult, especially during the middle years when family and work usually take more significant priority, yet for a more fulfilling, happier and longer life, it is definitely worth your effort.

The Benefits

Friendship can be an amazing prescription to all forms of emotional and physical pain. In fact, according to some medical experts, friendship could boost a person's sense of purpose and belonging. It is also said to increase one's happiness, decrease stress, enhance self-worth and assist you in coping with traumas, like serious illness, divorce, loss of employment or death of a person's loved one. That is why it is no longer surprising what a lot of people are greatly valuing their friends, and usually turn and go to their first during the times of predicaments, even before relatives or spouses.

The benefits on emotional health you acquire from your friends could also give some effects to your physical health. Based on some studies, social interactions could help you ease harmful stress levels that can potentially harm the arteries of your heart, insulin regulation, immune system, and gut function. In addition to this, having your friends around can also improve your immune system and can encourage you to recuperate from a devastating injury. To simply state, having good friends can do well to your health.

Even though the benefits of friendship could come naturally, usually, friendship does not. It could be very hard to locate people having similar values and interests. This is particularly true during the stage of adulthood, where responsibilities such as education, family, and career can greatly restrict your social life. That is why, if you know you find the true friends worth for you to treasure, keeping and making a regular connection with them should be observed.

CHAPTER 8

STAYING MOTIVATED FOR MAINTAINING FRIENDSHIPS

Synopsis

As said in the earlier chapter, if you know that your friends are true to you thinking that they are the ones worth keeping and staying with, then make sure you know the ways on how to maintain your friendships. However, before you can do this, you first need to stay motivated for maintaining your friendships.

If you wish to stay motivated at keeping your friends, you need to think about the reasons why you want to keep them. You can think about the precious memories both of your have shared during the good and the bad times. Having a friend to whom you share some of the memorable moments in your life could be very rewarding. Thinking about losing that person is never a healthy idea, so you will surely for your friendship to stay as long as you are living. Keeping this friend for a lifetime should be what you like.

This can be one way to keep yourself motivated about keeping your friendship.

Thinking how important your friend to you is also another way for you to stay motivated. You may imagine how you will feel once this friend has gone away, which will give you the will to keep in track of your friendship. Similar to any other relationships, a friendship also require some time and effort in order to maintain them helping them grow. So, if you want just that knowing how you to maintain your friendships should be your first step to take.

Showing some appreciation can be one way to keep good friends. There are times that when you've known the person for quite a long time, you start from taking him for granted. This must not be the case. Always make sure to thank a friend whenever he/she does a thing for you. Consider returning favors when friends make their way just to help you. Show them that they are not forgotten by their thoughtful friend, you. You can let them know they are not forgotten by offering them simple, yet appreciative things. Tell your friends how much you appreciate their existence, and that you are thankful they've come into your life.

CHAPTER 9

STAYING ON TRACK

Synopsis

If you really wish to maintain your friendship, you have to stay on track of it. As mentioned in the previous chapters, friendship is as important as any other relationships. That is why focusing on it could be a good idea. Staying on the track of friendship will help you maintain the relationship for as long as you want to.

Wanting to stay on track of the friendship, you need to display your interest in the life of your friend. A true friendship must be two-sided, so your friend has to show his interest in you just the way you show yours.

If you are focusing on your friendship, you will be a good listener when he needs you to be one. Being a good listener whenever your friend is talking about something that is happening in his life could be a good sign that you are interested of what he does.

Supporting Friends

Fine relationships are often established on communication. Hence, make sure not to disregard your friend. Take enough time to truly hear what he is saying, and only give advice when he asks you to. Your interest must always come with your support to your friend.

You can show your support to him if he is involved in a certain activity which he really puts his interest. For instance, if your friend is a basketball player, you can at least show him that you support him by appearing on his games. This could be a great way to keep your friendship on track.

Finding time to see each other and having fun together will not only help you stay on track of your friendship, yet it will also help you build a lasting relationship.

Considering this may be quite obvious, yet there are times when some people are trapped of simply using their friends to get emotional support and neglect the time to enjoying the company of one another. You may consider doing the things that both of you enjoy together.

Maintaining a fairly regular connection with your friend should help you stay on track. If your friend moves a far place from the one you stay at, make sure to keep a connection. Usually, people decide to move in order to attend to different school or continue their new career.

This does not mean that the friendships need to end. Contact your friend from time to time. If you are not seeing one another often, it is essential to monitor in order for you to be aware of the things happening in the life of your friend. Having a friend from a distant place might let you find it difficult to show his importance to you. You may do this by sending him greeting cards or some simple yet special presents that will let him feel how important your friendship is to you.

You can even send him the traditional letter writing, as this display how much effort you've exerted just for him to remember you. Friends are important, so doing this must not do any hardship on your part.

CHAPTER 10

MAKING RESOLUTIONS FOR FRIENDSHIPS

The coming New Year will probably carry with it the inspiration of changing your life in which your friends should be a huge part of it. In spite of everything, don't you think your friends are the ones who let you make the most of your life? If not, it is then the perfect time for you to determine the types of friends you have. Perhaps it is them, or perhaps it is you. Either way, you should consider making the best resolutions for your friendships this coming New Year.

Getting rid of your toxic friends should be considered if you wish to have a healthy relationship. Call them whatever you like, "frenemies", emotional vampires or simply toxic vampires. These people are the ones consistently bringing you down on which they even let you have negative thoughts about friendship. Spending much of your time with this type of people might skew you about the real meaning of a good friend. Whatever you may like, you confront them, stay away from them, or simply move on. Begin your New Year having the fresh attitude of letting good people enter into your life.

Make and spend some time with your friends. Busyness is one of the biggest relationship slayers. So, if you want to remain friendship with your good friends, finding time to bond with them should be a great resolution. These days, people's schedules are very jam-packed on which sometimes seeing your friends becomes very difficult instead a thing that you should be looking forward to. It is then time to reorganize your priorities, while the beginning of the New Year is an ideal time to accomplish it. A simple way to do this is through organizing habitual friendship dates. These should not be a very big deal, as it could be very simple like sipping a coffee or meeting your friend in a store. Your main point here should involve seeing and talking with your friend personally.

Thinking about and praying for your friends is another good thing to include in your New Year's resolution. Even if you are not actually spending time together, you can at least send positive thoughts your friend's way.

Having thoughts of other people can help you place your personal troubles within perspective, making you sentient of the alterations in the demeanor or moods of your friend. This could be a good way to show how much you care, although you are not together. Hence, pray for the goods of your friend by actively wanting the best for them. You friend might not know you've done it, yet such action could bring some changes on your mindset regarding relationships within your life, which in turn makes you a more empathetic friend.

Therefore, if you wish to make the most of your friendships, creating the most favorable and positive resolutions this coming year should be your first move to take. You definitely have acquired some of the possible friendship resolutions worth considering, so you may think about including them in your list.

9 786069 835876

Printed by Libri Plureos GmbH in Hamburg,
Germany